Love Learned, Gained, and Lost

Deborah Ackerman

BookLeaf Publishing

India | USA | UK

Presentation by *BookLeaf Publishing*

Web: www.bookleafpub.com

E-mail: info@bookleafpub.com

ISBN: 9789363316539

First edition 2024

To all of the loves through out my life. This book wouldn't be possible without you.

Luke

Full of hope
Magic and dreams
Times with you
Meant everything
Your eyes of green
Hair of chestnut
My first baby
Silenced so young
Burden with pain
Such an amazing boy
Trapped in chains
Heart of Jesus
Voice of love
My gift that returned above

Isaiah

Hair of David
Eyes of ocean
Heart of mischief
Love so pure
Smile of sunshine
Touch of wholeness
Spirit of Faith
One look at you is all that it takes

Montana

3

Fierce
Bold
Beautiful
Wise
Soulful
Laughter
Tears
Proud
No Fear

Home

The place of home
Distant now
A longing deep inside
My heart lives in the midst
My spirit further north

Youth

Wonder and hope
Bright with dreams
Amongst the neighboring houses
As far as I could see
Kids running and chatting
Mingling across yards
You'll forever live in my mind
Hopeful, laughing, scheming

Never

Wondered through the door
My eyes set on the screen
Turning to discover you
It wasn't what it seemed
Seared in my heart and mind
Kind, strong, and generous
But you'll never be mine

Text

A text of feeling
But nothing learned
Yearning endlessly
But never heard
A mix of sorrow
And delight at the sight
Of your name glowing
Lighting up my screen

Fast

A glit in your eye
The click in my soul
Quick to fall
Slow to speak
My missing piece
Perfectly shaped
Misaligning stars
Craving what I cannot possess

Distant

Choking silence
Hard to breathe
My heart for you
It's everything
Across the divide
My love must go
Frightened and excited
Into the unknown

Glance

Here in a flash
Gone the next
My heart remembers
Your voice with my name
Joy and fear
Love and regret
Present one day and lost the next

Freedom

Liberty at your lips
Floating on your kiss
Content in your arms
Fear of you leaving
Missing all that I gain
All as close as the mention of your name

June

Revival
Fall
Love
Fate
Hope
Peace
Joy
Second chance

Dog

Body of fur
Heart of gold
Love so young
Continues even when old
Paws of sandpaper
Ears of cotton
Eyes of joy
Forever my good boy

Break

14

Lingering pain
Heart shattered here
Left to pick the pieces
You left at my feet
Forced to repair
Never fit the same

Jesus

With my brokenness and sin
You looked down and called me friend
In my despair and fear
You still caught each of my tears
Forever to serve
Never alone
You make my life with You feel like home

Sister

Not by blood
Or by sport
You came to my life
By a choice
One that brought us together
Through thick and thin
Your light, your soul
I'm happy to call kindred

Brother

Strong
True
Annoying
Secure
Games
Adventure
Protection
Years gone
Time passed
A connection that will always last

Connect

By soul
Or body
Heart or mind
Time or distance
Cannot hide
Intertwined
Your name comes to mind
A love hoped to obtain
Across the plains of yesterday